101 FINISHING TOUCHES

Published by
BBC Books, BBC Worldwide Ltd
Woodlands, 80 Wood Lane
London W12 0TT

First published for Marks & Spencer in 2004

This edition published in 2006

ISBN 0563 49324 0

Commissioning Editor: Vivien Bowler
Project Editor: Deirdre O'Reilly
Series Design: Claire Wood
Book Design: Kathryn Gammon
Design Manager: Annette Peppis
Production Controller: Arlene Alexander

Set in Amasis MT and ITC Officina Sans
Printed and bound in Italy by LEGO SpA
Colour origination by Butler and Tanner Ltd.

BBC
BOOKS

101 FINISHING TOUCHES
STYLISH HOME IDEAS

Julie Savill

GoodHomes
magazine

CONTENTS

INTRODUCTION

Some people just seem to have the happy knack of being able to sling a few apparently unrelated things on to a shelf, somehow making an eye-catching arrangement. Or of always choosing the perfect picture and then getting it in just the right place to show it off to best effect. And then there's the rest of us…

While we might have an eye for a nice buy it's not enough to fill your home with attractive bits and pieces. What makes the difference between clutter and a collection is the way you choose to arrange and display the items and that's where this nifty little book comes in.

101 Finishing Touches is packed with the sort of ideas that professional stylists use every day of their working lives to set the style seal on their rooms. Display is a large part of that, knowing what will grab attention and how to give extra oomph to treasured but tiny things that, alone, would be lost and overlooked. Customisation is another key to style success. It's the ability to take a plain cushion or curtain and give it a twist that sets it firmly in the designer bracket but without a hefty price tag attached.

All the stylists at *Good Homes* magazine have heaps of ideas for little design details and believe that their finishing touches should be quick, affordable and easy. If you've got guests arriving in an hour, you're not going to get out the paint can and change the colour of the sitting room, but you might be tempted to fold a fresh throw to hide the shabby sofa, arrange a few pieces of cream china on the mantelpiece and pop some fresh-from-the-garden flowers into a vase to give your room a new and welcoming look.

Good Homes magazine has been lucky enough to have some of the best stylists in the business working for it and many of them have contributed the ideas within this book. Special thanks go to Lynsey Fryers, Sasha Stramentov, Ali Brown, Wendy Uren, Andrea Maflin, Sasha Cohen, Claudia Bryant, Petra Boase, Philip Clarke, Lucyina Moodie and talented florist Jane Packer. Many of the designers from the hugely successful BBC television home programmes are also regular contributors to the magazine and Brigid Calderhead and Handy Andy Kane deserve special mention. I would also like to mention Sophie Robinson, the rather fabulous home editor of *Good Homes* from 2002 to 2004. Many of the ideas within this book are the result of her enthusiasm and energy.

Julie Savill, Editor
May 1998 – June 2003

Shelf life

A picture shelf gives you the flexibility to change your display as often as the mood takes you. Frames of different sizes look great grouped together and the big advantage is there are no nail holes to be filled when you change the pictures on show. A box frame is a lovely way to show off mementoes or favourite pictures. Here, a family seaside shot is enhanced by the addition of a few shells gathered on a beachcombing expedition. You might also want to write a small label noting the time, place and people in the photo and stick it under the image. Among the frames on your shelf add other items to make a varied display. A junk-shop find like a glass, for instance, with a few leaves and one or two blooms trailing over the rim, small ornaments, candles and special birthday cards can all add to the interest.

TIP
Strips of picture shelf can be joined to stretch the entire length of the room if you want to make an impactful display.

Line 'em up

Narrow spaces call for special treatments. Now, you could just hang a group of pictures individually but that involves accurate measuring and lots of jiggling with picture wires to make sure the spaces between the frames are equal. A much easier idea all round is to take a series of budget wooden frames, paint them in different tones to complement your wall colour then hook them all together using screw-in hooks and eyes.

Measure 2.5cm in from either side of the top and bottom of each frame and mark a point. Screw eyes into the top edge of each frame and hooks into the bottom of all but the final picture in the row. Now you just need two screws in the wall to hook your chain of pictures onto. This idea works best with lightweight frames. If you are concerned about the weight, try leaving out the glass or replacing it with an acrylic sheet.

Spaced out

OK, so your pictures are beautifully framed but how do you get them looking good in a group? The general rule is that either all the top or all the bottom edges line up or that they make an overall square or rectangle. This is almost impossible to do if you are hanging the pictures on the wall and trying to create the grouping at the same time. Instead, arrange your frames on the floor as you want them to appear on the wall, then cut newspaper to the same size as each frame. On each piece of paper mark the hanging point (where the nail will need to be in the wall) then, using low-tack masking tape fix each piece of paper to the wall to match the layout on the floor. Hammer in picture hooks at the crosses, remove the paper and hang the pictures. For large pictures use hooks with two nails so you can be sure they'll take the weight.

Off the hook

It's not just what you hang; how you hang it is almost as important and can certainly be the thing that makes or breaks a simple picture. Instead of simply whacking a few picture hooks into the wall, consider decorative hooks and fixings. Tieback hooks, for instance, come in a whole range of decorative styles from high Victorian to chicly modern. And of course if you've got a fixing that's worth looking at you want to hang your picture in a way to show it to its best advantage. String, chain, ribbon or wool can all be used to suspend pictures from attractive hooks. Fix a small screw eye to the back of the frame at each side and simply tie onto it. These small frames gain in impact by being hung as a pair from large-headed nails. Bigger pictures would look good suspended from something with a bit more bulk, such as wooden door knobs.

Small is beautiful

Every home seems to have a collection of odd tiny photos, left over from ID cards or that last passport renewal, kicking around in a box or drawer. Taken in private, in those little curtained booths, these throwaway snaps often catch more character than formally posed shots so it's a shame to see them going to waste. Alone they are fairly insignificant but with the right treatment they can shine. What's called for is a statement frame – big, bold and eye-catching, and in a colour to contrast with your wall. Have a mount cut to hold one, two or a dozen tiny portraits and simply stick the photos to the back with masking tape. Once framed up and in pride of place on the wall they will get the attention they deserve. When framing things together try to stick to a theme so group black-and-white images in one frame, coloured images in another.

Cheap chic

Clip frames are cheap as chips and just the ticket if you've got a lot of things to frame. If the effect is just too 'student bedsit' for your liking add your own personal finishing touches to give them a whole new lease of life. Simply cutting a piece of fabric or wrapping paper to the size of the frame (use the glass as a template) and sandwiching it under the photo in the frame will make a world of difference. Choose a fabric to tone with your room scheme (this is where to use up those leftover bits of furnishing material). Think laterally for other ideas to create themes to match your images. Brown paper, dried leaves, metal foil or corrugated cardboard would all make a statement when teamed with the right pictures.

TIP
Pictures don't have to be central in a frame so twist and turn the image to see what effects you can create.

Back to front

Can't make your mind up about what to frame, or perhaps you need to flatter two sets of people? Take a standard frame with a mount and replace the backing board with a second sheet of glass. Have a second mount cut to match the original, but perhaps in a different colour and you're ready to get framing. Lay the frame face down with the original mount in place. Choose two sets of photos and stick them back to back. Place over the apertures in the mount and secure with tiny pieces of masking tape at the corners. Add the second mount face up, put the new glass back in place and fix with small pins. Now you can simply flip it to reveal a different set of images.

TIP
All your pictures will need to be either landscape or portrait to make this idea work.

Clearly simple

Some pictures are just so perfect that they need no fancy framing or hanging techniques. When you've got a set of photos that you just can't wait to get on the wall this is simplicity itself. You'll need a few clear plastic folders, bulldog clips in either clear acrylic or chrome and some suckers with hooks. Stick the suckers to a wall (they work best on gloss paint), a door or the outside of the fridge. Slip the photos in the folders and grip a bulldog clip to the top. Hang from hooks and enjoy! Black-and-white images photocopy beautifully and it's a cheap way to get big enlargements of your favourite pictures. This is fine with your own pictures but copyrighted images should not be photocopied for any reason.

TIP
If you are having photocopies made at your local copy shop ask about other services. Many can put pictures onto canvas panels, mugs and even mouse mats!

Tie a ribbon

Small pictures on a large expanse of wall need a little extra help if they are to hold their own and look anything other than lost. Grouping them helps but only if the frames or the picture subjects make them a natural match. With just one or two pictures it's still possible to pack a bigger punch if you use a little creativity in the way you hang them. Broad satin ribbon in a colour to tone in with the images is a good start. Tie it to metal screw eyes in the back of the frame, adjusting it for length so a reasonable amount will be seen when the picture is on the wall. Tie it off securely and loop the ribbon over a nail or picture hook in the wall. Hide the hook by gluing a large decorative button over the top as a final flourish.

TIP
Mother-of-pearl buttons in interesting shapes go with almost any colour scheme and add a little shimmer. Look out for them in jars of old buttons at car-boot sales.

Make for the border

Wallpaper borders used in the traditional way at dado rail height have fallen somewhat out of fashion but, used creatively, they can still be a big asset in a room. A favourite picture can be given extra prominence and presence by surrounding it with a wallpaper border frame that's glued to the wall. Hang your picture, measure and cut a length of border for each side then mitre the corners so they meet neatly. Paste the back of each piece, leave to soak for the time recommended on the packaging of the border then apply to the wall, brushing with a wallpaper brush to smooth it down and get rid of bubbles. If you have two or more pictures to hang you could either make individual borders for each or hang them as a group and run one large border around the lot to contain them.

TIP

To make neat mitres, lay the border pieces out in a square, overlapping the corners. Mark a 45 degree line at each corner and, using a sharp craft knife, cut through both layers of paper. Remove the two offcut corners and you'll be left with a perfectly matching mitre.

Free art

Next time you wallpaper a room be sure to keep any wallpaper samples you have collected while pulling your scheme together. They are likely to fall automatically into a colour family and will look great framed in quickly customised frames and hung as a group. To enhance your free art prime the frames in white, then paint them a soft colour to tone or contrast with your walls.

Rub over the dry surface with a candle and apply a top coat – you may need two to get a solid coat of colour if you are using a pale shade. When completely dry, sand the frames lightly to reveal highlights of the white coat underneath. A coat of clear furniture wax applied over the top and buffed off will give a sheeny, durable finish.

TIP
Try this with wrapping papers or remnants of furnishing or even dressmaking fabrics.

A family affair

Family photos can be overwhelming *en masse* but there's no need to tuck them away in an album. Rather than ranking the frames on a mantelpiece or sideboard, adapt a favourite Victorian display trick and make it modern. Large, fussy ribbon bows topping pictures used to be the order of the day but could easily overwhelm a simple, modern room. Instead hang your pictures from a ribbon banner. Staple the ribbon to the back of each frame, sew a D-ring to the top to hang it and cut a notch in the bottom to neaten and stop it fraying. If your frames are not suitable to staple into, hang the ribbon, mark where you want the pictures and tap picture hooks through the ribbon into the wall at the marked spots. Hang the pictures on the hooks as normal.

TIP
Layer different colours and widths of ribbon to match the shades of your room's colour scheme.

Off the rails

With today's passion for original features in older houses it's surprising that more people don't make proper use of their picture rails. The joy of hanging frames from hooks on the picture rail is that you can change what you hang and where you hang it as often as you like without damaging your walls. Picture hooks are widely available from large DIY stores and come in bright brass, aged bronze and even chrome to suit all sorts of decorating styles. To hang pictures you'll need to fix small metal screw eyes into the back of the frame. Then you need to choose your cord. Thick button thread, narrow ribbon, chain (fine for small images, thicker for larger ones) or silky upholstery cord all give a different effect. A common mistake with hanging pictures in this way is to have them on miserly short cords so they look throttled up tight against the picture rail. Don't be mean – you can always shorten the cord to raise a picture, so start long and stand back to check the effect.

The bigger picture

Little pictures need a bit of TLC if they are to be displayed with any degree of success. Individually they have little hope of catching the eye or holding attention but *en masse* it's a different story. Treating fifteen or twenty pictures as one is the way forward and will give them much more appeal. Make one large frame on the wall using lengths of dado rail with their ends cut to 45 degrees. Mark out the position for the frame on the wall and fix each length of rail in place using masonry nails. Use filler for any gaps between the frame and the wall and to fill over the nail heads. When dry sand smooth then paint the frame and the wall within it in a colour two or three shades darker than the wall. Hang your photos inside in a selection of clip frames or other simple barely-there frames.

TIP
This is at its best using black-and-white photos. Copy colour photos on a black-and-white photocopier to keep them within the theme.

Mirror, mirror...

A collection of small hand mirrors is quite tricky to display on a flat surface but really comes into its own on a wall. By mixing one or two ornate or traditional mirrors in amongst a group of cheap and cheerful modern acrylic versions the effect is contemporary but characterful and would work in any style of home. Use double-sided adhesive sticky pads on the backs of the mirrors to attach them to the wall, but be wary of doing this with a valued or valuable mirror as it could damage the surface. Instead wrap a soft satin ribbon around the handle and tie to secure, then loop this over a small pin or hook in the wall. Although this kind of arrangement will never match a single, large mirror for its light-reflecting and space-enhancing properties it will bring a freshness and charm to a room.

TIP
Small hand mirrors – particularly older ones – can be quite pricey but you can get a similar effect by putting mirrored glass into a mismatched collection of photo frames.

Add some sparkle

Fairy lights are for life, not just for Christmas. There's something a little magical about the effect they can bring to a room so don't pack them away on twelfth night but find a new home for them where you can enjoy them all year round. Looped around a large mirror over a dining table they will add a pretty glow and, while the effect is slightly eccentric with red bulbs, they could easily be changed for cool white or rich gold. Start and finish your light loop at the centre of the bottom edge of the mirror so the lead can go straight down the wall. A carefully arranged vase of flowers or bowl of fruit will hide the wires. This would also work along a mantelpiece or even over a door. Hold the lights in place with self-adhesive hooks in clear plastic, which are widely available at Christmas.

TIP
Flowers are especially effective in front of a mirror as, reflected in the glass, they give the impression of twice as many blooms.

Join the panel

A special piece of fabric is almost wasted being made into furnishings but comes into its own used as a wall hanging. Suspended from a pole it can make a stylish focal point in an otherwise featureless room. Lightweight fabrics will hang better if they are lined to give them a bit more body and stop them looking limp. Cut lining to the same size as your fabric panel, lay them face to face and stitch a seam along two sides and the bottom edge. Turn the panel through to the right side and sew a channel along the top edge which will slip over a slim curtain rod. Hang it from two hooks in the wall. Given the same treatment a treasured piece of clothing such as a silk kimono makes a strong statement. Slip a curtain rod through the sleeves so it is well supported and hang as before.

TIP
A collection of outgrown baby clothes suspended from a peg rail on tiny hangers is a sweet decoration for a toddler's room.

Lacy looks

Hand-worked table linen in fine crochet or lace is great fun to collect on your travels and makes a beautiful display. When you have gathered five or six pieces, lay them out on a table and rearrange them until you are happy with the layout, then start transferring them to the wall. Use slim panel pins and place them carefully through the holes in the lacework to minimise any damage. Tap the pins into the wall and hide the ends with tiny pearly buttons simply glued into place. Soft or very fine fabrics will be easier to hang and will keep their shape better if you starch them first. Use spray starch if you don't want to wash the items. To hang embroidered cotton or linen that doesn't have holes for the pins you might want to stitch a length of cotton binding across the back to make a channel for a curtain wire or narrow rod.

TIP
A hot glue gun is ideal for sticking fiddly things such as the little buttons on the pins as it sets fairly quickly and is quite precise.

Unlock your style

Rusty old keys are intriguing – just what did they unlock in the past? One key on a wall would look lost but a small group, hung on equally rusty nails or hooks, makes a magical collection. To give them more prominence paint a pale stripe or panel on the wall and arrange the keys within. They look best if the arrangement is left loose and casual rather than trying to line them up in regimented fashion. Old keys such as these can be picked up at boot sales and house clearances but you can age newer keys to give a similar effect. Put shiny, silvery or brass keys into vinegar and leave them for a few days. You'll find the acid dulls the surface and gives a pleasing aged look. Do the same thing with the hooks or nails from which the keys are to hang.

TIP
If the hooks have a protective lacquer try holding them in the flame of a gas hob or a lighter for a few minutes to damage the coating and let the acid get to work.

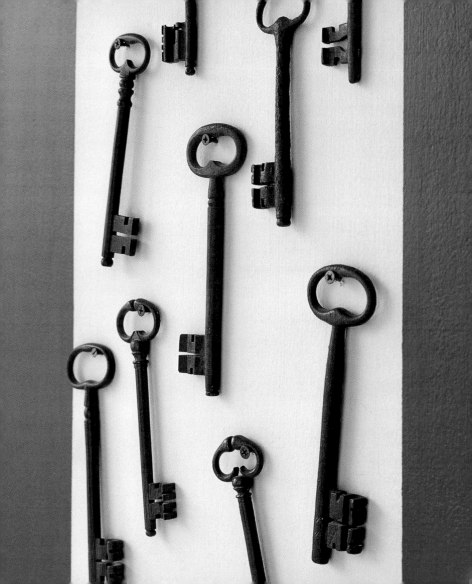

Mat finish

Flat baskets and coasters are hugely useful but not especially memorable on their own. But taken out of the cupboard and clustered together on a wall they make quite an impact in a kitchen or dining room. Hang them from tiny pins and they will still be available for their original purpose at a moment's notice. The secret to creating a successful display with everyday objects like this is to add some variety. An off-the-shelf set of six place mats will look dull and lazy, while a variety of items, some completely flat, some slightly dished, with and without handles, round and rectangular, looks as if the collection has grown over time with each item being specially chosen. Colour also helps to vary the effect so a couple of darker items amongst a group of pale straw baskets will help heighten the interest factor of your display.

TIP
French cheeses often come packed on small straw trays which are ideal for this type of display.

Fan club

One of the most tempting purchases on a trip to the Far East is the huge array of fans in exotic colours and patterns. Give in to that temptation and bring home an armful and you'll have a lavish, colourful and, above all, cheap display for a feature wall. Even if you're not off to such exotic destinations this year, paper fans are deliriously cheap to buy from shops specialising in Eastern imports. To hang a fan, make a small hole in one of the central ribs at the back, thread a loop of cotton or twine through and simply hang from a picture hook or small nail. The pleats in fans will mean they collect more than their fair share of dust. To clean them without damaging the paper use the small brush attachment on your vacuum cleaner and brush over them gently.

TIP
If you've been tempted by a more precious fan in painted silk or paper, it's best to have it framed in a custom-made fan case which keeps it clean and allows it to be displayed as a picture.

Can you handle it?

Inspiration for a display idea can come from the most unlikely source, as with this arrangement of door handles. Beautifully moulded in acrylic and in a dazzling range of colours they are special enough to take centre stage themselves. If such a modern look is not quite to your liking then think of the delights of wooden, brass and painted china handles that can be found in junk shops and at antique fairs. Arranged on a wall or the back of a door they offer the added bonus that the odd hanging item can be stored on them. An orderly row of these handles would also make an attractive alternative to a traditional peg rail and provide the perfect place to keep handbags, necklaces or children's clothes neatly to hand.

TIP
To fix the handles to the wall, use one of the extra-strong DIY adhesives such as No More Nails.

So gilty

There's something wonderfully indulgent, extravagant and appealing about heavily moulded gilt frames and buying one can begin a habit that's hard to break. Reproduction-carved frames are just as lovely as antiques and a lot more affordable. They make a show-stopping collection when grouped on a wall and the good news is that you don't need to buy the art to fill them as they are striking enough in their own right. Hang the frames in a random arrangement on the wall and then add little finishing touches to a few. A postcard stuck to the wall in one, a small frame hung inside a large one, a gilt butterfly or an old key all add to the slightly eccentric feel of the display. Keep the balance so there are more empty frames than full ones to keep the attention on the decorative carving and gilding.

TIP
A new make-up brush or shaving brush is the ideal thing to dust heavily carved frames such as these.

Style on a plate

Large plates and platters can be pressed into service in a kitchen or dining room to make a stylish statement on a wall. If the plates are of no special value it's fine to use regular wire and spring plate hooks to hang them. Lengths of plaid ribbon wrapped around will disguise the hooks and give a decorative flourish to the plates. Use wire-edged ribbon for ease as it will stay put wherever you want it without having to be secured. More valuable plates should not be mounted on wire hangers as they can chip the edges and reduce the value considerably. Instead, pay a visit to a specialist china outlet and buy adhesive plate hangers. You simply moisten the fabric discs, leave to go tacky then apply to the back of the plate. Once completely dry they are incredibly strong and have a D-ring attached for hanging.

TIP
Check the load for adhesive plate hangers and if you have a very large object to hang use two, side by side.

Remember when...

There's a fine line to be walked when displaying very personal mementoes if you're going to avoid an overly sentimental, slushy effect. But some things, such as a baby's first shoes, pictures of your parents as children or the first Christmas decoration you bought as a couple (that symbol of 'forever-togetherness') are just so important that they deserve to be seen but kept safe at the same time. One trick is to use a small hanging rail, suspended from two hooks in the wall and then simply add whichever items you want. Use a selection of toning ribbons in different widths and tie, hook, sew or stick your display to them. Knot the ribbons loosely to the rail and avoid bows at all costs. The beauty of this is that the display can be changed and you can have the pleasure of rediscovering old souvenirs tucked away in the back of a cupboard.

TIP
This would be especially pretty using antique ribbons that you've sought out from junk shops.

Spell it out

Oversized letters in gold or silver have become a popular mantelpiece decoration but there are diverse ways to use them and give them a bit more of an individual personality. Most are made of wood so it's simple to tap a couple of small nails in the back and string a wire between them to hang them on the wall. A fun idea that has been used to great effect in this bathroom is to collect enough of these letters, in different styles and sizes if you like, to spell out a word or phrase. Choose something appropriate to the place where it will hang – 'splash' seemed ideal here and is guaranteed to raise a smile. Of course you don't have to stick to decorative gilded letters. An extra quirky touch has been added here by using a celebration cake tin in the shape of the letter 'A'.

TIP
You might like to coat gilded letters with spray varnish before hanging them in a steamy atmosphere like a bathroom as the moisture could tarnish the metal.

Hide and chic

In the middle of winter, with flames leaping, a fireplace is the heart of any room scheme, providing a focal point, light and movement. But when the weather warms up and there's no need for a blaze, that central feature becomes a dead black hole. What's called for is a little scene setting to give it new character for spring and summer. The fire basket makes a natural container for an arrangement, and one that can be changed on a whim. A pile of garden twigs makes a rustic base while a gilded 'A' and a large star add a touch of glamour, but a heap of fir cones, a group of large church candles or a pile of pebbles would be equally pleasing. A fireplace that's never in use has even more need for a little stylish dressing. A pile of (unbreakable) baubles with a string of fairy lights woven through would give a shot of pizzazz at Christmas.

Spring fresh

Hyacinths are spring's best-value home-styling tool. The flowers last ages, the soft colours are uplifting after the gloom of winter and one pot will send its scent breezing all over the house. Buy them as dry bulbs or potted up and just showing some green (garden centres are the safest bet if you have your heart set on a particular colour). Pot up the dry bulbs and transfer growing bulbs from their plastic pots to wholesome terracotta.

Keep them somewhere cool and light and when the buds just start to show colour move them to the area where you want to display them. The warmth of the room will bring them into full flower in just a few days. Lined up on a dining room mantelpiece they look a treat if you tie a pale green ribbon around the pot and intersperse the plants with wine glasses full of sugared almonds which can be handed round after dinner.

TIP
After flowering, plant hyacinths out in the garden where they will flower away quite happily year after year.

Lean looks

Tradition would have it that pictures and mirrors have to be hung from the wall, but why? A very contemporary effect can be achieved by propping pictures on narrow shelves or, as here, on a mantelpiece.

This picture of a yacht in full sail has been appropriately surrounded by beachcomber finds such as pebbles and pieces of worn driftwood, along with contemporary ceramics in pebbly colours and textures. Try not to arrange things with too much symmetry as it can look forced and self-conscious. Placing the picture off-centre leaves room at one side for the taller vases and flowers without obscuring the image. The addition of a candle brings a whole new look to the display when it's lit in the evening.

This kind of arrangement of favourite personal items not only works as a display but as a reminder of days out and places visited and can be added to or changed as the mood takes you.

TIP
Change the display to reflect the passing of the seasons. This is a summery setting but with a more autumnal picture and a collection of, say, dried leaves, fir cones and a tiny pumpkin or two the mood created would be entirely different.

Modern mantelpiece

The plainest of plastered fireplaces needs sympathetic styling if it's not to be over-whelmed. A few ceramics in whites and blues arranged in little groups fill the space and add interest but don't fall into the trap of being too regimented and symmetrical. A variety of heights on a mantel shelf is pleasing but avoid a roller-coaster effect where tall things are interspersed with short leading the eye up and down. Here, one large vase dominates with its wild profusion of spring flowers, while the remaining objects are more restrained, being of similar height, colour and size. Above the fireplace, in the place of a traditional picture is an altogether more modern paint effect. The ghostly rectangles have a subtle impact and have been created by masking off shapes and then lightly brushing small amounts of paint off the masking tape and onto the wall. Build up the effect gradually to avoid a clumsy result.

TIP
For more drama, try the brushed wall effect with metallic paints that catch the light beautifully.

Pearly queens

The narrow space on a mantelpiece does impose some restrictions on what you can display there, and how it can be arranged. Large vases of flowers will only look top-heavy and precarious so something lighter and more delicate is called for. With one bunch of ranunculus or similar long-stemmed summer flower you can make a pretty arrangement that's at its best in a plain, pale room. Take half a dozen narrow vases of differing heights (or different sizes of drinking glass), pop two or three stems into each and top up with water. Float imitation pearls in the water to give an individual twist. Buy these cheaply from haberdashers or cut up an old junk-shop necklace. Some of the beads will sink and others will float, held aloft by the bubble of air caught in the thread hole. Range the vases along the mantelpiece for a romantic effect.

TIP
To encourage tight-closed ranunculus to open, re-cut the stems and place them in warm water with some flower food.

On the right trail

How you treat a mantelpiece can extend to more than just what you stand on the shelf. If you take a creative approach to dealing with the wall above, the whole chimney breast becomes a key feature in the room. In this sitting room a pretty crushed berry shade has been chosen for the walls but with the simple curtains, plain furniture and large but quite severe fireplace the overall effect would be unwelcoming were it not for the joyful freehand pattern on the wall. Added as an afterthought, this stencilled fringe of trailing leaves in pure white gives a more relaxed, laid-back atmosphere to the room and links with the crisp white of the fire surround itself. Against this exuberant backdrop the only additional adornment the mantel shelf needs is a few shapely monochrome accessories, arranged as one cluster rather than straggling across the whole width.

Beat the clock

When time is short and there's a table to be dressed, park your pride and get down to some serious cheating. Bold statements are easier to organise in a few minutes than small fiddly details so think big. For flowers, buy an arrangement that comes ready tied so all you have to do is whip off the cellophane and drop them in a sparkling-clean glass vase. To give them a lift and add a splash of individuality, fill the vase with fruits or small glass beads submerged in the water. Crab apples, kumquats or limes are all ideal and you can choose something to tone with the colours of your flowers. To finish the arrangement take a few fruits, push thin wire through one side and twist to make a stem. Push the stem into the centre of the bouquet to hold the fruit in place.

TIP
If using sizeable apples you can secure them by pushing toffee apple sticks into the fruit and wedging them firmly into the arrangement.

Effortless arrangements

When you're trying to do a stylish supper for six, complicated flower arranging can seem like just too much effort. Well, as luck would have it, there's no need to get into anything tricky with florist's foam and pins as current trends in flowers are for simple, relaxed arrangements that need almost no effort. Flowers for tables should be low so they don't get in the way of eye contact and conversation, so a saucer is the ideal container. Place a pretty jam jar or small glass in the middle of the saucer and pour water into it and around it. Pick the heads off summer flowers and lay them in the water in the saucer then float a tealight in the glass to make a centrepiece. A row of these twinkling down the centre of the table costs little and looks very attractive.

TIP
This is a great way to get a little extra value from the last few surviving heads from a large arrangement or bouquet that's past its best.

Ring the changes

If you shop cleverly, one set of china can be made to do duty for all sorts of occasions. What you're looking for is the tableware equivalent of the little black dress: something not too showy for everyday use, that will look classic and timeless teamed with natural-linen napkins for a family Sunday lunch but that can be jazzed up with the right accessories to look the part for a posh supper with friends. Jewelled napkin rings are just the thing to ring the changes and you can make sets in two or three colours to set a different scene. Take a 1m length of jewellery wire and thread one bead on as far as the centre. Fold the wire in half and twist together, trapping the bead. Thread both wire ends through more beads and tie the wires in a half knot to secure them. Twist the wires together for 16cm then thread more beads onto the other end. Twist wires to secure the final bead.

TIP
Check out car-boot sales for old necklaces at around a pound a time and use the vintage beads for style on a budget.

Top tables

Couples with kids may find it easier to get together for Sunday lunch when the children can join in and there's no need for a baby-sitter. Keep things simple by cooking dishes that everyone can dip into at the table rather than dishing up everything in the kitchen. That way all the china you need can be ready and waiting on the table and looking gorgeous when everyone arrives. If you have a smart table use place mats rather than a table-cloth and stack plates, bowls and napkins at each setting. A fabric runner down the centre sets a more modern note than a formal cloth and is more in keeping with the relaxed mood of a meal with mates. Look out for offcuts of fabric that can be picked up quite cheaply and simply hemmed. If you can't sew, use iron-on webbing.

TIP
Set a separate small table for children using bright colours, balloons tied to the backs of chairs and unbreakable picnicware.

Faking it

While artificial flowers aren't everyone's cup of tea arranged in a vase and masquerading as the real thing, they do a fantastic job as a last-minute life-saver when you're trying to create a pretty table scene. Against a backdrop of a plain wooden table and the most unassuming of white china, all it takes is some decorative napkin rings to give each place setting a colourful twist. Take a spray of silk flowers and snip off individual flower heads with their stems. Twist the wired stem around the front of the napkin ring, making sure the end of the stem ends up inside the ring. Use a different flower colour at each place setting and coordinate with matching napkins in different tones. You could take this a step further and decorate the stems of wine glasses to match and if you use a different flower for each glass at a party everyone will know which is their drink.

TIP
If your flowers aren't on wired stems push a length of thin wire through the back of the flower head, twist the ends of the wire together and wrap onto the napkin rings.

Do the twist

Setting a table for a special meal is the perfect opportunity to explore different textures. Set glistening ceramics and glassware on chunky woven linens and mats for a pleasing play on surfaces. With the emphasis on texture, colour becomes a secondary tool that you can use sparingly to add highlights here and there. Crunchy, freshly laundered linen napkins placed in a bowl at each setting need just a twist of ribbon to spark a party mood. Choose a wired ribbon that can be secured in a simple knot and tease the ends into shapely ruffles. For the price of a couple of metres of ribbon you can ring the changes with the colour for different occasions. Try a hint of rosy pink or a dash of orange against a dark-wood table and sage green or aubergine with lighter woods, then match the colour to a display of fruit or flowers for the centre of the table.

All for one

This clever idea needs a little time investment initially, but once you've made the mats it takes a matter of minutes to set a seriously stylish table each time. Cut a piece of fabric (we used fashionable faux suede) about 32 × 26cm for each place mat. Press and stitch a narrow hem all around. Cut another piece of fabric 17 × 13cm, press under a small hem all around and stitch the top hem of the pocket. Stitch the pocket to the place mat around the remaining three sides, lining up the bottom of the pocket with the row of stitching on the place mat. Slip the cutlery for the place setting inside the pocket and set the lot on the table. Use a narrow trimming of the faux suede to tie around each napkin. This is a great way to entice children to help setting the table – they love filling the pockets with cutlery.

TIP
For this idea, choose washable fabrics that don't fray.

Throwaway style

For sheer ease and economy you can't beat paper place mats as a way to put a finishing touch on a table. Choose your paper and cut it to size, allowing enough space all round for cutlery and glasses. If you're feeling especially keen you could use pinking shears or cut the edges into scallops but there's really no need. Best of all with this idea is there's no need to wash and iron the mats after use – if they're dirty, just throw them away; if they're still clean, save them for next time. Of course, if you've gone to the expense of a beautiful hand-made paper that you truly love then you might want to go one step further and have the place mats laminated to make them wipe-clean and reusable. Most local photocopy shops offer this service and it should still work out cheaper than shop-bought mats.

TIP
If you do keep the mats to use another time store them flat rather than rolling them up.

A glass act

Anyone who's passionate about their home should have a collection on the go, not with the aim of filling their home with tin soldiers or old farm tools, but to amass little groups of things that just introduce an extra bit of personality. Part of the charm of these collections is that they can't simply be bought off the shelf and that care and effort have gone into their creation, but it also gives a purpose to those weekend strolls around junk shops and the like if you have one eye out for something special. A collection of pressed glass is a brilliant place to start – it's affordable, available and makes a beautiful summer table setting for afternoon tea or a light supper. From plates to candlesticks, if everything on the table is glass allow yourself one flourish of colour. A generous bunch of ruby sweet peas, for instance, tumbled into a bowl – glass, of course...

Candle dice

This is a great way to use up pieces of wood left over from other projects and make something truly useful into the bargain. Cut the wood down into cubes of about 10cm. On each face of each cube mark two diagonal lines from corner to corner. Measure the diameters of a taper candle, a dinner candle and a small church candle. Starting with the smallest, take a wood drill bit the same diameter and make a 2cm deep hole at the centre on one side of each cube. Repeat with drill bits that match the size of the other candles. Sand the wood blocks smooth then give them a coat of furniture wax to bring them up to a sheeny finish. Choose a colour of wax to tone with other woods in your room. These look great in a row down the centre of a table with a random mixture of candle sizes burning in them.

On the slate

When you've got a beautiful wooden dining table, heat-proof place mats are an essential. And even when you're using a tablecloth they will help protect the wood underneath and catch many drips and spills that make washing white linen or damask a challenge. Large roof slates make ideal place mats – they're long so there's plenty of room for cutlery on the side, they're wipe-clean and they will handle the hottest plates with ease. Rub a small amount of Danish oil into the surface to give a sheeny finish. Check out the haberdashery section of your local department store where you'll find self-adhesive green felt circles in varying sizes which are ideal for sticking on the back to stop the slate scratching polished surfaces. More slates can be cut into squares to make matching coasters. To complement the natural theme of the place mats, put a small (clean) pebble at each setting.

TIP
Wipe the slate place mats clean by hand and do not put them in the dishwasher.

Go with the throw

Pale sofas are a tempting proposition while the fashion is for light and airy interiors but they are a magnet for spills and marks. If you've chosen a suite with loose covers that go in the machine, top marks for practicality. If not, you need a few clever tricks to disguise the damage and give a little extra visual interest. The days of the all-over throw hiding an old or marked sofa are well gone. Today's smart way to use a throw is to fold it neatly and use it as a banner over the back and seat or wrapped neatly over the arm. This way it can be positioned to hide a stain but your sofa still keeps its tailored good looks. Add an armful of cushions in a mix of subtle patterns and textures and not only your sofa, but your room will be transformed. Throw in one or two covers in long-haired Mongolian wool, felt or velvet for real feel-appeal.

TIP
If you're buying a sofa with fixed covers it is worth every penny to have it treated against staining when you buy it. Ask your retailer if they offer this service.

Button it!

If you're looking for anything but the most basic cushions you'll already know that something interesting with a quirky, modern touch generally has an interestingly high price tag to match. It is, however, simplicity itself to add a little quick customisation and lift everyday shop-bought items into an altogether more stylish league. The easiest place to start is with a bag of buttons, which you can pick up for next to nothing at jumble and car-boot sales. A single large button in the centre of a square cushion or a neat line of them along the middle of a rectangular one will give an expensive-looking hand-crafted finish. Instead of sewing them on in the usual way, these have been tied on with thick button thread. Using a large-eyed needle, take the thread through the button to the back of the fabric then back through the other hole to the front. Tie the ends and cut fairly short.

TIP
If you find the thread comes untied, a little blob of clear adhesive in the centre of each knot will secure it.

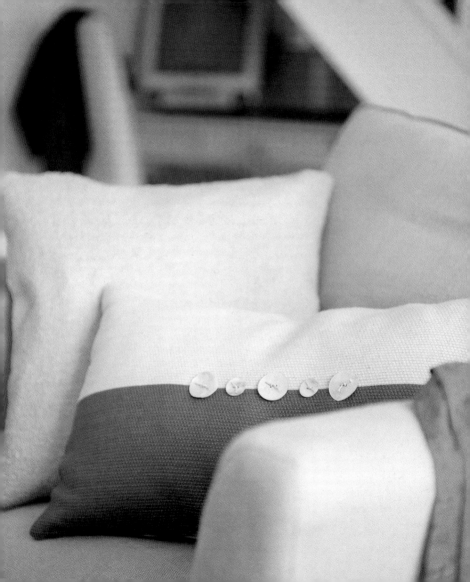

Under cover

There's something almost irresistible about the remnants box in a fabric shop with all those one- or two-metre lengths of material at rock-bottom prices that look as if they will come in very useful one day. Five minutes spent rummaging is almost always rewarded with one or two pieces to squirrel away and if you have a collection of fabrics you always have the means to rustle up a little decorative finishing touch for a room. These bolster covers are the perfect example. They need just one line of stitching and take a few minutes but look a million dollars in silk or taffeta. Measure the circumference of your bolster and cut a piece of fabric to fit around it, allowing for a seam. Stitch the fabric into a tube. If you use the full width of the fabric you won't need to hem the ends as the selvedge won't fray. Slip the bolster into the cover and knot the ends for an easy but decorative effect.

TIP
Fabric not wide enough to knot the ends? Tie with matching ribbon or cord.

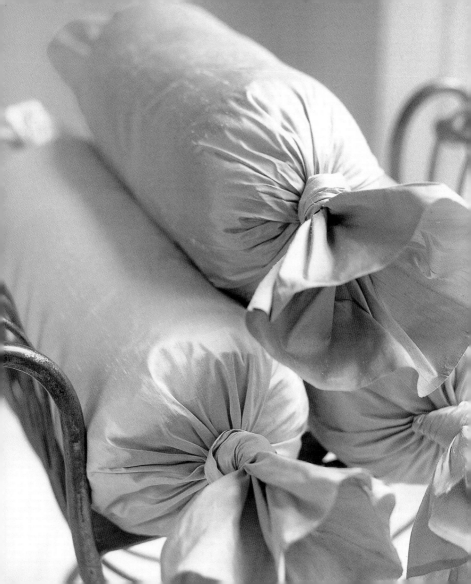

Ribbons and bows

If your style is unashamedly pretty the vintage chic look will be just up your street. Layering spriggy, floral prints on walls and bed creates a girly, feminine feel that works well with ribbon trimmings. In this room a simple roll-up blind has been refreshed with new ribbon ties in a contrasting colour. To copy the effect, cut four lengths of ribbon the full length of the blind. Stitch two to the front of the blind and two to the back, roll the bottom of the blind up to whatever level you like and tie each pair in a neat bow. A row of tiny African violets in pots with matching saucers completes the delicate scene. This look could be adapted for a rustic country room by using raffia or string to tie the blind up.

TIP

In a more clean-cut modern room, rather than securing the ties with a bow, add a button and loop to the ribbons for a more tailored look.

Best seats in the house

If you have dining chairs with fabric-covered seats mealtimes can soon take their toll, especially if there are children and chocolate involved! Drop-in seats are the best option here as it takes very little to change the fabric and give the chairs a whole new look when they're looking tired or if you change your colour scheme. Remove the seat from the chair and take off the old fabric using pliers to pull out any tacks or staples. Use the old fabric as a pattern to cut new pieces. Lay the fabric, right side down, with the seat pad on top. Starting at the centre of one edge, wrap the fabric over the edge of the seat and staple or tack in place. Repeat along the opposite side, working from the centre out to the corners, pulling the fabric taut and smooth. Fix the sides in the same way, neatly pleating the corners.

TIP
Check when you choose your fabric that it meets current fire regulations for upholstery.

Heads you win

Upholstered headboards strike a pretty note but fixed covers become grubby over a period of time. If you have a staple gun it's a simple job to whip up a new cover from a piece of upholstery fabric. Choose a fabric that's at least as wide as the headboard to avoid seams and cut it roughly to size, allowing enough material all round to wrap to the back. Starting at the centre top, wrap the fabric over, making sure any pattern or motif is centred, and staple it to the back. Work from the centre outwards, stapling as you go and turning under the side edges to neaten. Repeat along the bottom edge, pulling the fabric taut to keep the pattern straight. Once the fabric is firmly stapled in place you can neaten the back by covering it with a piece of lining fabric held in place with upholstery tacks, lightly tapped into place. Fold the raw edges under as you go.

All tied up

Formal tiebacks are not high fashion at the moment but the fact is that there are times when you want or need to hold a curtain aside to let in more light or stop it obstructing the view. There's lots of fun to be had with your choice of tieback style and you can make it match or contrast with the style of your room. In a crisply tailored room furnished with pinstripes and woollen fabrics, a nod in the direction of men's clothing seemed appropriate, so a length of ribbon was worked into a tie knot around the curtain and the ends cut to points. In a more feminine room an old beaded necklace might be brought into play or a length of twine threaded with drilled shells for a rustic scheme. All that's then needed is a small hook screwed into the wall over which to loop your chosen tieback.

TIP
Keep tiebacks on the low side – around a third of the height of the curtain from the floor – for a slouchy, modern feel.

Shine on

As far as curtains go there's masses of choice at the moment for anyone who wants to cut out the sewing machine and go the ready-made route. Sheers and semi-sheers are highly fashionable right now but because there are so many of them on the high street and because so many people now have them they're in danger of becoming a bit tired. A little no-sew customisation will go a long way to keeping them looking fresh, individual and modern. Wide bands of iron-on sequins are available at good haberdashery departments and they can be used as they are in stylish plain bands or cut into narrower strips or shapes as the mood takes you. Mark on the curtain where you want them to be (this is most easily done by folding the curtain and lightly ironing a crease into it). Line the sequins up and press them into place – simple!

TIP
If you can't find iron-on sequins use wide embroidered ribbon and attach it with Bondaweb.

Custom finish

Anyone doing up a home on a tight budget should remember one little designer secret: the magic of budget basics. Almost anything you can think of from tableware to bedlinen can be found in plain and simple ranges for a fraction of the price of their fancier, patterned counterparts. The trick to turning these brilliant basics into stylish furnishings is in the little twists you add yourself. Take this blind, for instance. It cost just a few pounds and was bought off the shelf and ready to cut to size. But, with the addition of a single strand of ribbon glued along the lower edge and a row of pearly buttons stuck on top, it looks a million dollars. Stitch a similar row of ribbon and buttons along the top edge of a plain dyed duvet cover or on a pair of pillowcases and you've got designer style on a shoestring.

TIP
If your duvet has a button
fastening on the opening
replace those buttons
with pearly ones to match.

Screen saver

In a kitchen that doubles as a diner it's a challenge to keep clutter under control and create a relaxed atmosphere for dining. Hanging a series of white roller blinds from the ceiling allows you to pull them down in front of the wall cupboards to worktop level when you've finished cooking so all your pots and pans, gadgets and bowls are out of sight while you enjoy a chilled-out supper with friends. With the under-cupboard lights switched off and the room lights dimmed it's a masterful disguise that changes the whole atmosphere of the room in an instant. This is also a great way to tidy up open shelving if you're tired of having everything on permanent display. Hang the blind from the top of the shelves or from the ceiling above and roll it down to hide things away – it will also help to stop items stored on shelves getting so dusty.

TIP
A floor-length cloth gives immediate glamour to a workaday kitchen table when entertaining.

Change the bed

In less than an hour you can change the look of your plainest bedlinen and give it some real designer cachet. No good with a needle? No problem. Fabric glues are quick, easy and make a washable bond that will last. Simply measure the top edge of your duvet cover and the open end of a pillowcase and cut pieces of fabric to trim them. Turn under the edges by about 1cm and iron flat for a neat finish. Apply a thin line of fabric adhesive along the sides following the manufacturer's instructions, lay the trimming strip in place on the duvet cover or pillowcase and smooth down firmly. Leave to dry to form a firm bond. The current trends for bedrooms include silky textures and embroidered fabrics so choose trimmings to reflect these styles. Strips of ribbon would also work a treat.

TIP
If you choose a fabric that you think might shrink wash it before using it to trim your linens.

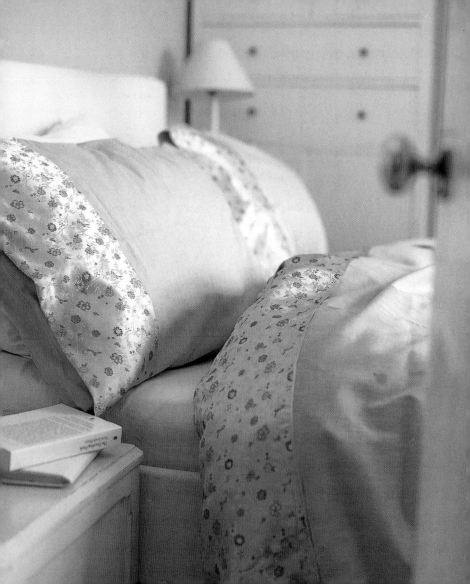

Handle with flair

A well-designed handle that's a pleasure to look at and comfortable to use can be the making of a door or piece of furniture. But handles don't have to be chosen just from the selection in the shops. In this kitchen a creative mind has been at work and wittily chose to reflect the cooking theme of the room in the replacement handles for the units. Wooden spoons can be picked up at bargain basement prices but look a million dollars in this context. The old handles have been removed and long screws inserted into the holes from inside the cupboard. These were then screwed lightly into the back of the wooden spoons to leave plenty of free space to get a good grip on the handle. To treat the handles wipe them over with a little ordinary olive oil or Danish oil.

TIP
Slip a small piece of plastic tubing over each screw to cover most of the thread before screwing it into the spoon. This will prevent you scratching your hand on the thread.

Fashion pack

Every season there will be a few key accessories that sum up the mood of the moment and are worn time after time. A beaded bag, some strappy sandals, a light cardigan – these are all the things that can lift an everyday outfit and give it that individual twist. And as they look so good it seems a shame to tuck them away in a cupboard or drawer between seasons. Instead, take a simple chrome kitchen rack and screw it to the back of your bedroom door. Add a few S-hooks and suddenly all the clutter is off the floor and making an eye-catching display too. One word of warning: a little personal restraint is called for here as this is not the place for last year's worn down kitten heels or your gardening cardie – to earn their place on this rail every item must be worth a closer look.

TIP
Hang out-of-season bags on the hooks and they become extra storage for scarves, belts and other small accessories.

Summer line up

Once the weather turns warmer you want to eke every last moment out of the balmy evenings. But it's not just the humans that like their evenings long and warm. Along with the summer come the insects. If you don't want to become a walking snack bar for mozzies, be prepared with a display of natural flickering candlelight interspersed with incense and citronella to ward them off. Use a thick string (or even the washing line) and simply peg small gauze bags containing citronella tealights and insect-repelling incense coils along its length, then add other little decorations such as pebbles and shells threaded onto strings. Make sure that the candles are hung on longish wires so their heat doesn't burn through the line. If you then dot other citronella candles around your garden seating area you and your friends should have a bite-free night lit by the flickering flames.

TIP
Been bitten? Rub with fresh marigold leaves or the juice from fresh parsley to ease the irritation.

Weight a while

When the days are warm enough it's a real treat to eat outdoors. Adding small weights to each corner of the tablecloth will stop the evening breezes lifting the tablecloth or flipping over the corners into the trifle. You can buy tablecloth weights ready made in a wide range of styles but it's simple – and quite fun – to make your own. First choose your weights to suit the style of your table setting. Here, pebbles have been used but you could try large metal washers, door knobs, tiny terracotta plant pots or even old spoons. Whatever you choose, wind a length of thin garden or jeweller's wire around and then bind the other end of the wire onto the hook of a cafe curtain clip making sure the ends of the wire are neatly finished to avoid snagging. Clip each weight onto the corner of the cloth but remember to remove them before laundering it!

TIP
Don't leave the clips outside overnight as damp will make them rust and they'll then stain your table linen.

Moth beaten

If you've ever had moths in your wardrobe you'll know just how much damage their tiny little larva can do to natural materials. Mothball has never rated highly on anyone's list of favourite scents but there are other ways of repelling them that add a fresh scent to all your clothes at the same time – bargain! Firstly, hanging your clothes on cedar-wood hangers will go a long way towards keeping moths at bay – they just hate the smell of the wood. Next, it's time for a little scented sachet that looks pretty and smells heavenly to you but definitely not to moths. Cut a square of fabric with pinking shears to stop it fraying and add some strips of dried orange peel and a few cloves. Pull the corners together and tie with a ribbon, allowing enough extra to form a loop to dangle the sachet from your hanger.

TIP
To dry orange peel, cut it into strips and place in a brown paper bag in the airing cupboard for a few days.

PRACTICAL TOUCHES

Frame fixer

There's no written rule that says a frame has to have a picture displayed in it. In fact, with a little modification a picture frame can be turned into a really useful little shelf that's as quirky and stylish as it is practical. Cut two wooden battens to run the width of your frame and screw in place top and bottom of the back making sure the bottom one lines up with the edge of the frame opening. Then cut a piece of wood or MDF to make the shelf and fix it in place by screwing down through the shelf into the wooden batten. Sand the frame and the shelf, give it a coat of primer and then one or two coats of eggshell. Hang it using mirror plates that screw to the back of the frame and hook over more screws in the wall.

TIP
This is a useful idea in a bathroom where space is tight or you could make a pair of shelves and hang them either side of a bed.

Hang it high

Think peg rail and you usually conjure up an image of a bedroom or possibly a kitchen. But in a small bathroom a peg rail is a bit of a boon for some quick storage. Either buy your peg rail ready made or create your own by screwing small wooden door knobs to a slim batten and screw it into place. All your everyday items like bath brushes and towels can find a home there but it's also a good idea to allocate a drawstring bag to each family member so all their personal bits and bobs get stashed out of sight and not left lying on the edge of the bath. A net bag is also good for bath toys. Hang your peg rail on the wall over the bath, pop the toys into the net after use and they'll carry on draining into the bath and be fresh and dry ready for next time.

TIP
Make everyone's drawstring bag in a different colour or pattern so they're instantly identifiable.

Stick with it

A finishing touch that makes life more beautiful is well worth the effort, but if it will also make life easier it surely deserves space in your home. Every kitchen has a drawer where bits and pieces of paper (receipts, old notes, cheques, phone numbers) get stuffed, but how much better would it be to have them on a board where they'll stay safe, clean and to hand? Thin sheet metal can now be bought at large DIY stores and it's up to you to decide how big a board your family needs. About 75cm × 50cm would make a good starting point. Glue the metal to a piece of plywood, place it in a frame to cover any sharp metal and hang with picture hangers screwed to the back and to the wall. Fix all your notes to the board with magnets.

TIP
Take a fridge magnet with you when you buy your sheet metal to make sure you choose something that it will stick to.

Frosty front

Clear glass doors on cupboards are all very well if you have beautiful things, neatly arranged inside. However, if you'd rather draw a veil over the contents of some of your cupboards, frosting is the way forward. This can be done in two ways: either with sticky-backed acrylic film from sign-writing shops, which you can use as it is or cut a design into, or with glass etching spray from DIY stores. To apply the film, cut it to fit each pane of glass, wet the glass with water and a drop of washing-up liquid, then slide the film into place, smoothing out any bubbles. If you're using the spray, draw a design onto the back of the glass with a rubber-based adhesive such as Copydex and leave to dry. Spray over it and leave to dry again then peel or rub off the glue to reveal a clear design.

TIP
The film and the spray are also useful in bathrooms. Frost the lower half of a window to provide privacy without blocking daylight.

Key to success

If you're forever putting keys down, making them more obvious might be one way to remember where they are. Adding a pretty tassel, bought or made from embroidery thread and beads, is one way and is a sweet finishing touch for a cupboard key when left hanging from the door. To make a tassel, wind two skeins of stranded embroidery thread around a 10cm square piece of card. Cut a 20cm length of embroidery thread, slip the wound thread off the card and loop the strand through the top; tie it to make a hanging loop and secure the top of the tassel. Use a short length of thread to tie around the top of the tassel just below the hanging loop. Snip through the loops at the bottom of the tassel and trim the ends level. Thread the hanging loop through three beads then tie in a knot to secure it. Attach to the key.

TIP
Make a key board by fitting a plain piece of wood into a decorative frame. Screw hooks into the front and paint the lot in your chosen colour. Hang your keys from the hooks with their coloured tassels attached.

Homely and handsome

For wholesome good looks you can't beat the appeal of nuts, pulses, pasta, sugar and flour displayed in glass jars. Getting all those everyday ingredients out of your cupboards and onto a shelf where you can see them will free more space for other less-than-lovely kitchen essentials to be hidden away. Kilner jars, usually used for bottling and preserving, are perfect containers for a country-style kitchen, they're dishwasher safe and cheap into the bargain. Buy them in lots of sizes and decant all your dried goods into them. Not only will they look good but they will last well and stay fresh for ages. You might find that after a year or so the rubber seals on the jars start to perish and split but replacements are readily available. Staying with the country theme, keep a small collection of wooden scoops for spooning the contents out of the jars.

TIP
Don't forget to snip the cooking instructions off the packets of more unusual ingredients and drop them in the top of the jar so you can refer back to them.

Step change

Using something out of context for an altogether different purpose can have a very charming effect. The ability to see a new use for something can come in extremely useful when you find yourself without a key piece of furniture or accessory. In the absence of a suitable bedside table this little set of kitchen steps has been pressed into use, with the top step providing a home for a plant, a cup of tea and a nightlight, while the lower step is ideal for night-time reading material. Once you start looking at things afresh it gets you thinking about what else you could use for a different purpose. A wine cooler, for instance, makes a great utensil holder, a dressing table doubles as a desk if you're working on a laptop and an old kitchen chair makes a great plant stand in the garden.

TIP
To be user-friendly, a bedside table should be about 5–10cm taller than the mattress height of the bed.

The latest soap

There's nothing much to be said in favour of a washing-up liquid bottle sitting alongside the sink – it's just not pretty! But it's too much hassle to keep putting it out of sight in the cupboard, so what's to be done? Decanting liquids into oil drizzlers and recycled glass bottles is a great way to create a bright, light touch and make these everyday items into a kitchen plus point.

Washing-up liquid, dishwasher rinse aid and liquid hand soap can all be decanted in this way and the different colours make a pretty sight. Can't remember what's in each one? Hang aluminium or copper garden plant tags as labels round the necks. Write on the tag with a ballpoint pen and it engraves the word into the metal to make a long-lasting label.

TIP
As with all household cleaning products make sure these are safely out of reach of small children – not least of all because the bottles are glass and will break if dropped.

Sign language

A glass panel in a bathroom door does wonders for the light levels in a dark hallway but is a complete loss when it comes to privacy. A clever compromise is to resort to frosting which will let the light through and preserve your modesty. You could just treat the glass with frosting spray and be done with it but there's an opportunity here to do something a little more engaging. To create a word or message in the frosting print out your chosen letters, at the size you want, from a computer. Stick them together with equal spacing between the letters and tape them to the back of the glass panel. Ensure the glass is clean and dry, stick a piece of clear, self-adhesive film to the front, covering all the letters and carefully cut around them with a scalpel. Peel away the excess film, leaving just the letters and spray with frosting as usual. When dry peel away the letters to reveal your word in clear glass.

TIP
Don't forget to mask off the door around the glass with newspaper before using the frosting spray.

bath

DECORATIVE DETAILS   Taper trick

The most satisfying finishing touch is one that costs little or nothing but delivers plenty of impact. A few well-worn pebbles with natural holes in them make ideal holders for tiny candles. While one on its own might look lost, a small cluster gives a charming breath of seaside style to a bathroom windowsill. Here, they partner a taller, wire candle holder but white candles have been used throughout to link the different materials. It's not recommended to take pebbles from beaches but bags of garden pebbles often yield ones with holes or depressions big enough to take a slender taper. Alternatively you could drill holes in smooth pebbles using a masonry drill bit and setting the drill to a slow speed. If the holes in the pebbles are large, wrap the base of the candle in a blob of Plasticine to make it fit snugly and safely.

TIP
Pebbles with holes that go all the way through should be placed on a saucer or tray to stop wax dripping through onto the surface of your furniture.

Plant power

The trick when displaying a group of items is to make sure they are linked by at least one thing. That linking element might be colour, shape or material. A row of houseplants, for instance, has all the more impact if you choose leafy green plants that are grown for their foliage rather than flowers. The effect is enhanced by the fact that each plant sits in a silvery metallic bucket or pot. They're not all the same but they work because they have something in common. This trick of repetition also works to make very cheap items look impressive. Buy one cheap thing and it will look, well, cheap. Buy three or five and the effect will be bold, confident and stylish. Elsewhere in the room family pictures, some in colour, some black-and-white, have been linked by framing them all in pale beechwood frames to match the furniture.

TIP
It is always easier to make an odd-numbered group of things into a pleasing arrangement. Somehow twos and fours of an item can look unhappy and stilted, whereas threes and fives look at ease and natural.

Pot luck

In spring when potted bulbs are plentiful and cheap in markets and garden centres take full advantage to make cheery indoor flower arrangements. The plastic pots they come in are unlikely to match your style values but rather than spend time and money repotting, take the quick and easy route. A large leaf from a house or garden plant makes a stylish wrapper and the way you secure it can be tailored to your room scheme. In a country setting a twist of raffia or hairy string tied in a relaxed knot is just the ticket, while for more urban surroundings a leather bootlace or even a silver bulldog clip might be the order of the day. No suitable leaves? A scrap of leftover fabric, wrapping paper or even brown parcel paper could be pressed successfully into service. Oh, and don't be mean with the bulbs – try buying in threes and lining them up or setting them out in a group with flowers at varying heights.

TIP
Waxy leaves make the best wrappers as they will last several days before drying out.

Egg shell shades

It seems that wherever you go on holiday you can usually find decorated real eggs and artificial 'eggs' made of stone, enamel or even metal. These little souvenirs make a pretty display grouped on a plate or in a shallow dish and are a daily reminder of places visited. A quicker way of getting a similar effect is to blow hens' or ducks' eggs and dye them in a range of soft colours. To blow an egg make a 2 or 3mm hole in the round end and a pinhole in the pointed end using a needle. Push the needle into the egg to break up the yolk and make it easier to blow. Put your mouth to the pinhole and start blowing hard with a bowl underneath to catch the egg. When the egg is empty, rinse the shell in cold water. To dye the shells put a generous dash of food colouring into boiling water and steep the shells for around 10 minutes.

TIP
Some supermarkets sell Cotswold Legbar eggs which naturally come in a range of colours from buff to pale blue, khaki and olive green, saving you the trouble of dying them!

Take a tassel

Sometimes a plain and simple piece of furniture can earn its place in your home just by virtue of its practicality, but with the minimum of expense and effort the dullest piece can be refreshed and revived to give it an elegant look to match. This handy bedside table offers bags of storage for guests but, with mean wooden knobs, was looking very dated. Removing the knobs and replacing them with slightly frivolous tassel handles has brought it right up to date and given it a new lease of life with a dash of wit. The loops at the top of the tassels were fed through the original handle screw-holes, slipped through a metal washer and knotted to secure.

TIP
If your tassels are too long and dangle over the drawer below put a band of tape around the tassel at the length you want it and cut along the bottom edge of the tape. This will ensure you get an even line when you cut.

Pram power

First impressions (or what estate agents call 'kerb appeal') can make or break someone's impression of your home. It's a vital thing when you're selling as many buyers are put off before they even set foot inside a property. Even if you're not on the move this is a great way to give your front garden the wow factor. Unusual containers brimming with summer plants are show-stoppers and none more so than this traditional old pram overflowing with petunias and daisies. To make this look work, line the pram with black plastic, fill with a suitable compost and plant into it. Alternatively, fill the pram with bedding plants still in their pots so you can replace fading plants with fresh new blooms through-out the summer. Geraniums, pelargoniums, ivies and pansies would all thrive in this setting. Choose blooms in one or two colours for a coordinated effect and make sure you mix one or two trailers with the more upright varieties so they will sprawl lazily over the edge.

TIP
Mixing water-retaining granules with the compost will keep your display looking fresh longer and reduce the number of times you need to water it.

DECORATIVE DETAILS

Which switch?

When you've put a lot of effort into decorating and furnishing your home it's the small details that can make or break the final effect. If you give as much consideration to the tiny things as you have to the wall colours and the shape of the sofa, the room will have a professional polish. One thing that lets down many a home is the plain white switches and sockets. Against coloured walls they stand out when you would much prefer they just blended into the background. There's a wealth of decorative switches and sockets available in metals and coloured plastics from high-street outlets and DIY sheds and these take just a few minutes to fit. If you're not confident about your wiring skills look out for the versions that are designed to slip simply over your existing fittings.

TIP
Clear acrylic switch surrounds are widely available and let the wall colour show through for a seamless effect.

DECORATIVE DETAILS   China syndrome

A display of china is one of those lovely old-fashioned styling ideas that can be reinvented to fit into any type of home, no matter how modern. Traditionally it would have been arranged on a dresser, but if you don't have the space for such a thing a set of shelves can make just as pretty a display. Fix a length of narrow beading to the front of each shelf to stop plates sliding off then start your arrangement. A more homely, cottagey effect is achieved by mixing the pieces of china, so instead of having a whole row of dinner plates, then another shelf of teaplates, intermingle plates, bowls, cups and saucers to give a range of sizes and shapes on each shelf. The china shown here is from one dinner set that incorporates two different-coloured backgrounds but such a display would work with any mismatched collection of ceramics as long as you choose a colour scheme – and stick to it!

TIP
A small blob of Blu-Tak on the back will hold a cup or plate at just the angle you want it.

Home office

Working from home puts extra pressure on your storage space. Files and folders, computer equipment and books all need a home and if you don't have space for an office these have to be incorporated into another room somehow. Open shelving, while providing bags of storage space, can be a bit of an eyesore if it's packed top to bottom with paperwork, so what's needed is a quick disguise. Hanging a ready-made curtain panel over the front is the solution. Attach it at the top with Velcro (one half sews to the curtain, the other sticks to the shelving) then make a narrow channel at the bottom and slip a length of dowelling through to weight the curtain and hold it in place. When you need to work the curtain is easily pulled aside or removed altogether simply by detaching the Velcro.

TIP
Paint the wall and the bookcase the same colour and dye the curtain a similar shade and it will all fade into the background and be less obtrusive.

Glass distinction

If you like something - no, let's go further than that - if you really love something it's fine to buy in bulk. A range of eye-catching Venetian-style glassware, with its different sizes and mix of frames and mirrors, makes a terrific display when grouped on a mantelpiece. This type of glass has enjoyed a burst of popularity recently and affordable copies are quite widely available on the high street. Something as pretty and decorative as this could be made to work in different ways. First, as here, it makes a lovely mixed arrangement with family photos in the frames and one of the mirrors hanging on the wall behind. The loose arrangement of white ranunculus in a vase adds a softer note, but no colour, to the display. Alternatively, all the pieces could be hung from the wall with other glass, such as candleholders or a vase, on the shelf in front.

TIP
Look out for other items
of elaborately etched
glass to display alongside
Venetian-style frames.

Paint a-peel

If you have a piece of furniture that you're just not happy with, take a fresh look at it. If the shape is good and it's in OK condition then it's a prime candidate for a little quick reinvention. To give a piece of wooden furniture an aged, worn feel first clean it thoroughly and sand to give a key to the old finish and give it a coat of primer. Then comes the clever bit. Take a candle and rub it over the areas that would normally get the most wear – the edges of a table, around the handle of a cupboard or along the back of a chair. Paint the piece of furniture in your chosen top coat in either a gloss or, preferably, an eggshell finish. Once the paint is well and truly dry (leave it for at least 48 hours, longer if possible), sand lightly over the waxed areas where the paint will come away easily to reveal the colour of the wood underneath.

Instant ageing

The time-worn appeal of the shabby chic look means it just goes on and on gaining in popularity. The idea is to strike a balance and have things that look as if they have been loved and used for a lifetime rather than things that look as if they are on their last legs. Modern gilt frames can be very good value but are a bit eye-catchingly bright for this kind of faded look. However, a wash of white paint would soon have the newest of frames looking as if the gilt has peeled over the years to reveal the plaster-like Gesso underneath. Give the frame a light sanding with very fine grade sandpaper to give it a key. Then brush or wipe on a thin coat of eggshell in one of the 'old' white shades from one of the heritage paint ranges. Leave to dry and then, if there is still too much gold showing add another coat but leave it slightly patchy and uneven.

TIP
Put too much paint on? You can wipe it off with a soft cloth while it is still wet or leave it to dry and use very fine sandpaper to rub it back.

DECORATIVE DETAILS   Book order

Do your bookcases look a mess? Join the club! Take a few moments to do some nifty styling and you can turn your bookcase into a display in its own right. Arrange the books in groups rather than solid rows, using bookends to keep them neat and upright, and intersperse with plants, pictures and vases. Play around with the composition – if a coffee-table book has a gorgeous cover, bring it into view by propping it up facing forward like a picture. And don't be afraid to stack some books on their sides for a change. This can work as a little platform to display a small dish or tray, or as a bookend to stop other volumes falling over. It's also a clever way to get the odd too-tall book into the bookcase. You might need to take some books out of the bookcase to get it looking stylish but they can be used elsewhere in the room, in a little pile on the coffee table or on a footstool, for instance.

TIP
Be guided by the predominant colours of your books for the other items in your display. If there is a real mix of colours only add things in neutral colours and natural materials.

One for the pot

French confit pots, originally designed to hold preserved duck, are hugely collectable and sought-after. As a result they are becoming harder to find at affordable prices but they are the sort of thing that makes a wonderful collection and are worth the occasional splurge when you find another one. They come in all sorts of sizes, usually with the top half glazed in either ochre or green, and look their best when displayed as a mixed group. This sort of rustic, earthy item looks at home against old, well-used country timber furniture. If they are to be stood on polished wood or a painted surface put small discs of baize underneath to prevent scratching. In this collection one pot has been used as a planter but the others are left empty so they can be enjoyed in their own right.

TIP
As with all collectables, these confit pots gain in impact by being displayed as a group but, as they are quite chunky, no more than five at a time, please.

Paper backs

Repainting a junk-shop cupboard is a great way to give it a new lease of life and tie it in with your colour scheme. But why stop there? If you take a wallpaper to match or contrast with your scheme and use it to line the back of the cupboard it will make a real feature. If the shelves come out, remove them and paper the back of the cupboard in one or two straight drops. If not, you'll need to cut pieces to fit between each pair of shelves. Stick the paper in place with either wallpaper paste, spray adhesive such as Spray Mount or pin it with a border of drawing pins. This makes a lovely backdrop for a collection of pressed and cut glass or ceramics in white or plain colours. Alternatively, you could paper the shelves rather than the back of the cupboard for a slightly more subtle effect.

TIP
Try this in a cupboard with solid rather than glass doors for an unexpected flash of colour when the cupboard is opened.

Great crates

An old wooden crate, weathered and worn from years of use, makes an ideal container for an indoor display of herbs or aromatic plants. Line it with black polythene, and either fill with compost and plant it up or pack the plants, still in their pots, inside and surround with moss. Stacked with soft greeny-grey lavender and left on a low table it is an invitation to touch and the slightest brush will release the scent into the air. In the kitchen this is a terrific way to keep herbs growing long past the end of summer. Plant up the types with strong summer associations, such as basil, oregano and mint, leave the box near to a window so it gets maximum light and keep it watered. You'll enjoy those fresh sunshine flavours well into the autumn and your kitchen will benefit from the lush, leafy green of the growing plants.

TIP
Avoid over-watering as there is no drainage through the plastic lining of the box and Mediterranean plants such as lavender won't tolerate being waterlogged.

Light up your life

Despite the fact that home style is an intensely personal subject and the only thing that really matters is pleasing yourself, there are one or two basics that every home really should have. One of those is tealights. These brilliant little things are a complete life-saver when time is short and you just need an instant wow factor. Bought in bulk (get bags of 100 if you can – you'll always find a use for them) they cost pennies each so you can afford to be lavish. And it's that lavishness that turns these modest little candles into a real show-stopper. For an instant table centrepiece or garden light, take a large metal tray or shallow ceramic dish, add a centimetre or two of fine white sand and nestle a dozen or so tealights on top. Light them and there you go: a beautiful display in under five minutes.

TIP
Once well-lit, tealights become very hot and the sand will stop the heat transferring through the tray and burning the surface below.

Love leaves

As the seasons change it feels right to reflect that in some way in our homes. Small but well considered touches are easy to manage and can be all that's needed in a plainly decorated room. Leaves are an obvious emblem to mark the end of summer and the arrival of autumn. Pressed and dried they can be used to line platters for fruit or arranged in a frame but they will be brittle and won't stand up to too much handling.

Preserving leaves with a glycerine mixture keeps them flexible and colourful, giving you more ways to use them. Here a single highly coloured and shapely leaf has been fixed to the front of a tealight glass with an old-fashioned dolly peg so the light of the candle shines through. To preserve leaves to use in this way cut a small branch and stand in a mix of one part glycerine to two parts water for about three weeks.

TIP
Individual leaves
can be preserved by
immersing completely
in a 50:50 solution
of glycerine and water.

On reflection

If you are one of those people who has bits and pieces stashed away all over the house because they were left over from other jobs and looked too useful to throw away, congratulations, you have the perfect source of finishing touches. With a few odds and ends and a creative mind it's quite possible to make something spectacular out of the things that a more ruthless tidiness freak might have discarded. Take this mirror, for instance. It's been rustled up out of a single bathroom mirror tile and a slate that slid off the roof last winter – hardly the most glamorous of beginnings. The slate tile was sliced lengthways into four using a tile cutter then simply stuck around the edges of the mirror using a strong DIY adhesive. Here, it is simply propped atop a mantelpiece but if you wanted to hang it, it would need a square of plywood glued to the back of the mirror and small screw eyes fitted.

TIP
Single slates are widely available at salvage yards for about a pound each.

Twinkle, twinkle

For a piece of artwork that twinkles all year round it's time to dust off the Christmas fairy lights and give them a new starring role. Take a piece of 9mm MDF and drill a grid of holes just large enough to poke one of the bulbs through. Sand, prime and paint the board with emulsion then pop the lights through the holes from the back, holding them in place with small pieces of electrical tape. Fix a screw eye to each side at the back, run picture wire between them and hang the whole panel from a hook in the wall. If you prefer a more random, sky-at-night effect forget the grid and go freestyle. Just remember to drill the right number of holes for your string of lights. White lights are the go-with-anything choice here but you could use gold or the fabulous bright blue that's now widely available. Just one word of caution – the world might not be ready for this using multicoloured lights, OK?

TIP
This works brilliantly above a bed where the wire for the lights will be almost obscured by the bedhead.

Off with their heads

For outstanding value and sheer cheeriness there are not many flowers to rival the gerbera. Even when they're near the end and starting to droop their heads a little you can eke a bit extra out of them. Cut the stems down to 6–8cm, pop each flower into a separate votive holder and display them in ordered rows on a low surface. The rim of the glass will support the head and they'll last for a few days. This is a great way to make a very few flowers go a long way and works just as well with carnations, blowsy garden roses or even with pansies in tiny eggcups. Even with just two flowers you can make a stylish statement. Take two narrow drinking glasses of different heights, pop a flower stem in each and stand side by side on a mantelpiece. For extra impact add a couple of drops of food dye to the water.

TIP
Place the flowers on a mirror tile to increase the effect and bounce light up around them.

Press ahead

There are two ways to tackle ironing. One is grit your teeth, grab the iron and get stuck in and try to get the whole boring business over with as soon as possible. The other is to approach it with a bit more domestic-goddess goodness in your heart and try to make a wholesome, comforting ritual of it. Scent plays a huge part in creating atmosphere in your home and will lift or soothe the spirits depending on the fragrance. The many scented linen waters that are available are worth every penny for the double pleasure they bring. There is something deeply satisfying about standing over a pile of crumpled linen and turning it into a neat stack of pressed sheets smelling of rose, lavender or verveine. The bonus is that when you come to use the sheets your bed will smell sweetly and the scent will help lull you to sleep.

TIP
Always put the linen water into a spray bottle and never directly into a steam iron.

DECORATIVE DETAILS   Tumbler trick

If you go to your kitchen cupboard right now it's a certainty that there will be two or three little glasses, the sole survivors of some set or other that has gradually been chipped or broken over the years. As odd drinking glasses they're not particularly useful but they can be reinvented quickly and easily to make a set of stylish votive holders. Take a piece of tissue paper and cut to size so it will wrap right around the glass.

Keep it about 2cm shorter than the height of the glass. Use PVA glue to stick it in place on the outside. Wrap a narrow ribbon around the top edge of the tissue and fix with more PVA. Glue a row of little shell buttons to one side, pop in a tealight and enjoy! Using different coloured tissue papers will give different effects – try pink or peachy shades in a dining room for a warming glow that will flatter the complexion.

TIP
Glue more buttons along the bottom edge of a blind, around the base of a light shade or to the frame of a mirror to pull a room's accessories together stylishly.

Give us a swirl

Revamping plain glass vases is easy and a great way to tie old accessories into a new colour scheme. Pour some enamel paint into the bottom of the vase and then swirl it around gently to make an asymmetric pattern. Sit the vase down and allow it to dry (a pool of paint will collect at the bottom so be patient and give it plenty of time). To make a design around the top edge of a vase, use the same technique but pour the paint just inside the rim of the vase while it rests on its side. Plenty of newspaper on the table is an excellent idea at this stage! Roll the vase around to spread the paint and the pour the excess out of the top. Leave the vase on its side to dry thoroughly. Choose a selection of toning shades for your vases and they'll look as good empty as they do with flowers.

TIP
Wash painted vases carefully and avoid using scourers.

It's a wrap

Not many of us have the cupboard space (let alone the budget) for different sets of tableware just for Christmas but with a little bit of effort even the most everyday set of stainless steel cutlery can become the star of the seasonal table. A reel of satin ribbon in a colour to coordinate with your china is what's called for. We went for go-with-anything white for its icy shimmer. Fasten one end of the ribbon to the handle with a small piece of double-sided tape, then start to wrap. Continue to the end then double back down the handle for about a centimetre. Secure the end with tape, then cut a piece of ribbon and tie a tiny bow around the handle to cover the end.

TIP
If you've really got the Christmas bug you could wrap each place setting in a different pastel colour and strew pastel-coloured baubles down the centre of the table.

On the fringe

This is such a simple idea you might be able to get the kids involved in making these icicle candle holders. Measure the circumference of a plain glass candle holder (a drinking tumbler would do just as well), then cut a strip of white tissue paper at least 3cm wide and long enough to go around the holder with a small overlap. Fold over around 1cm along the length of the strip then start cutting triangles into the wider part of the strip to make a toothed fringe. Wrap the tissue fringe around the candle holder and secure the ends with Pritt Stick or a small amount of double-sided tape. Fluff the points up so they stand out and then add further fringes of different widths – the more the merrier!

TIP
You might find it quicker to fold and snip long lengths of fringing then just cut it to fit the candle holder afterwards.

Memory garland

If time is the thing you've just run out of on Christmas Eve and some speedy styling is what's needed before the family arrive, treat yourself to a little rustic style. The natural look doesn't rely on hours of work to create a polished result but gains in charm from the use of wholesome materials and simple techniques. For a quick garland to adorn a mantelpiece or banister the ideal starting point is a ball of hairy parcel string. Raid the bottom of the decorations box for an assortment of odds and ends that won't make it on to the tree and start stringing. This is the perfect way to display those sentimental little reminders of Christmases past – the tag from a baby's first present or a decoration bought to mark an anniversary. Intersperse with kitchen storecupboard finds such as dried orange slices, bay leaves and cinnamon sticks.

TIP
To pack the garland to reuse next year wind it around a piece of stiff card to stop it tangling.

Pile on the style

If there's one thing that Christmas should never be it's mean. So when it's time to put up the decorations go for broke and really pile it on. Buying a few decorations each year will soon mean you have a big boxful to dip into each year. One thing that's worth splashing out on is a really good fake garland – not one of those cheap and wispy little things but a can't-tell-it-from-the-real-thing swag of greenery and cones a couple of metres long.

With this and a few fake flowers, a handful of baubles and about 30 minutes you can decorate your hall and be ready to welcome guests. Start at the bottom of the stairs, wrap a little fine wire around the end of the garland and secure to the newel post. Wind the garland up the handrail and secure the other end in the same way. Wire on a few fake flowers (big lilies are lovely) and some (unbreakable) baubles then stand back and admire!

TIP
Twine a set of white Christmas lights through the garland for a magical effect in the evenings.

Photo finish

When you've got a bunch of mates coming round for a post-Christmas lunch it's time to kick back and relax so a formal table setting would be just too stuffy. What's called for instead is a light, fresh feel with a touch of wit. Use a black-and-white Polaroid camera to snap your friends as they arrive then use the pictures as place cards. Punch a hole in one corner of the photo and tie to a shop-bought or home-made cracker with narrow velvet ribbon. If you like to have small table gifts at Christmas they could be included inside each cracker. Carefully open up one end of shop-bought crackers, ease the gift inside and close. In keeping with the black-and-white pictures keep the rest of the table monochrome with crisp white china and napkins, slate place mats and white flowers.

TIP
Customise shop-bought crackers to fit the black-and-white scheme by covering them in a delicate hand-made wrapping paper.

Candle magic

The Scandinavian look is perfect for today's modern, pared-down interiors. Simplicity is the key and busy details and overly fussy fabrics are stripped away so the little things have a chance to be noticed and appreciated. A line of plain white candles set into glass tumblers is effective, beautiful and easy to put together. Just drizzle a little candle wax into the base of each glass then stand the candle inside. Standing the tumblers in front of a mirror will make the light dance around the room and double the impact. Look out for tumblers with a little etched detailing around the rim which is all the decoration this simple arrangement needs. Filling the glasses halfway with water will mean the candles are automatically extinguished before they burn right down but, as with any candle display, this arrangement should not be left burning unattended.

TIP
Reusable candle putty is a Plasticine-like material that can be used to fix candles securely into any holder. Look out for it in specialist candle outlets.

Little wonder

There's something sweetly appealing about a miniature Christmas tree decked out in full seasonal regalia that's a bit like a child wearing its parent's shoes. Everything is oversized and rather out of proportion but somehow it only adds to the charm. Tiny trees that are the perfect size for hallway displays are readily available these days, usually ready-potted so there's no messy business. Just pop the pot into a decorative basket or tin, making sure there's a saucer inside to hold water if the tree is rooted. Set the tree in position and give it the full works including some full-size baubles for that *Alice in Wonderland* fantasy touch. Use more baubles in the same colours suspended from toning satin ribbons to jazz up the banister and loop beaded garlands underneath as a final flourish.

TIP
If you have playful cats or children, only attempt this banister treatment with baubles you know to be unbreakable.

Jugged flair

With a large glass jug or vase it takes a matter of moments to create a different table centrepiece for every day of the Christmas period if you want to ring the changes. For instant style, pile it high with a collection of sparkling baubles in colours to match your table setting. Make sure there are plenty of small ones or you'll end up with a jug with only three or four baubles inside, which isn't exactly the effect you're looking for. The easiest alternative would be to change the accent colour of the baubles, leaving all the silver ones but swapping the pink for green, for example. Other ways to fill the jug could include a mix of sweets in shiny metallic wrappers for people to dip into after dinner, flower heads submerged under water, marshmallows, floating candles or small fir cones sprayed in metallic shades.

TIP
A string of fairy lights piled into a glass vase or jug looks a treat twinkling away on a sideboard.

Send a message

When everyone's at home over Christmas it's nice to do one or two special things that you wouldn't normally have time for. Once all the last-minute wrapping is done on Christmas Eve and it's time to settle down to eat the mince pie and drink the sherry that was left out for you-know-who, you might find the energy to put a little personal touch on everyone's plate ready for that late and lazy Christmas breakfast. Setting the table the night before gets one more chore out of the way and these little decorations take barely a minute or two each to put together. At each setting put a glittery bauble into an egg cup. Write a tiny personal message in silver pen on a scrap of pastel tissue paper and fix it to the bauble with a flourish of silvery wire – done!

TIP
If you're feeling particularly well organised in the run-up to Christmas these could, of course, be done in advance...

STOCKISTS:

ART AND CRAFT EQUIPMENT

THE BEAD SHOP
Suppliers of beads and
jewellery-making accessories.
Tel: 020 7240 0931
www.beadworks.co.uk

BOSTIK
Good range of adhesives
including Sew Simple fabric
glue.
Tel: 01785 272727
www.bostik-findley.com

CANDLE MAKERS SUPPLIES
Suppliers of batik wax and
tools.
Tel: 020 7602 4031
www.candlemakers.co.uk

CREATIVE BEADCRAFT
Specialist company offering
a wide range of beads, sequins
and trimmings available by
mail order.
Tel: 01494 778818
www.creativebeadcraft.co.uk

DOVER STREET BOOKSHOP
Stockists of copyright-free
images for photocopying and
decoupage.
Tel: 020 7836 2111
www.doverbooks.co.uk

DYLON
Manufacturers of fabric dyes
in a wide range of colours,
suitable for both washing
machine and hand use.
Tel: 020 8663 4296
www.dylon.co.uk

HARVEY BAKER DESIGN
Wooden storage boxes and bins
that can be decorated at home.
Tel: 01434 685500

HAWKIN & CO
Suppliers of candle sand.
Tel: 01968 782536
www.hawkin.com

HOBBYCRAFT
Arts and crafts superstores
stocking a huge range of craft
materials.
Tel: 0800 027 2387
www.hobbycraft.co.uk

HOMECRAFTS DIRECT
Wide range of craft products
available by mail order.
Tel: 0116 269 7733
www.homecrafts.co.uk

JALI
Suppliers of MDF mouldings,
shelving, trims and flatpacks.
Tel: 01227 833333
www.jali.co.uk

L. CORNELISSEN & SON
Suppliers of a wide range of traditional artists' materials plus aluminium, silver and gold leaf and specialist tools for gilding.
Tel: 020 7636 1045
www.cornelissen.co.uk

LONDON GRAPHIC CENTRE
Specialist shop offering a range of design sundries, art and craft supplies plus a good selection of handmade papers.
Tel: 020 7759 4500
www.londongraphics.co.uk or www.lgc-online.co.uk/catalogue

PAPERCHASE
Modern and design-conscious stationery retailers offering a good range of wrapping and tissue papers, ribbons, twines plus cardboard and plastic boxes and containers suitable for storage.
Tel: 020 7467 6200 for branches or 0161 839 1500 for mail order
www.paperchase.co.uk

SCUMBLE GOOSIE
Ready-to-paint furniture and accessories including blanks for peg rails, trays and lampbases.
Tel: 01453 731305
www.scumblegoosie.co.uk

SPECIALIST CRAFTS
Makers of a wide range of craft products.
Tel: 0116 269 7711 for stockists or 0116 269 7733 for mail order
www.speccrafts.co.uk

THE STENCIL LIBRARY
Stencils and stencilling tools by mail order.
Tel: 01661 844844
www.stencil-library.com

THE STENCIL STORE
A wide range of stencils and specialist paints available by mail order or from branches nationwide.
Tel: 01923 285577
www.stencilstore.com

VV ROULEAUX
Extraordinarily wide range of haberdashery including ribbons, braids, cords, trimmings, beads, sequins, feathers and curtain tassels.
Online mail order available.
www.vvrouleaux.com

WOOLWORTHS
Stockists of Dylon fabric dyes plus a small range of craft basics such as glues, paint brushes and paints.
Tel: 01706 862789 for branches
www.woolworths.co.uk

FABRICS AND WALLPAPERS

ALMA HOME
Leather and suede available in a good range of colours.
Tel: 020 7377 0762
www.almahome.co.uk

ANDREW MARTIN
Printed fabrics and wallpapers, velvets, suedes and leather.
Tel: 020 7225 5100

ANNA FRENCH
Floral and paint-effect wallpapers; printed cotton fabrics, lace and sheers.
Tel: 020 7349 1099
www.annafrench.co.uk

BERWICK STREET CLOTH SHOP
Wide range of inexpensive fabrics including felts and latex plus a good selection of brightly coloured cotton voiles.
Tel: 020 7287 2881

CALICO
Sells everything from voiles and muslins to PVC-coated, tapestry and furnishing fabrics.
Tel: 029 2049 3020

CATH KIDSTON
Romantic 1950s-style floral prints with retro feel.
Tel: 020 7221 4000 for stockists or 020 7229 8000 for mail order
www.cathkidston.co.uk

CELESTIAL
An inspiring and unusual range of beaded trimmings and fringings.
Tel: 020 8341 2788
www.celestial-trim.com

COLEFAX & FOWLER
Beautiful florals on linen and chintz, and an extensive range of weaves and wallpapers.
Tel: 020 8877 6400

DESIGNERS GUILD
Colourful and contemporary fabric and soft furnishings.
Tel: 020 7893 7400
www.designersguild.com

THE FABRIC WAREHOUSE
Extensive ranges of furnishing fabrics.
Tel: 0800 316 4408
www.fabricwarehouse.co.uk

GRAHAM & BROWN

Contemporary wallcoverings, including textures and metallics.
Tel: 0800 328 8452
www.grahambrown.com

IAN MANKIN

Natural fabrics in plains, stripes and checks, including plenty of classic tickings and ginghams.
Tel: 020 7722 0997

JANE CHURCHILL FABRICS

Wallpapers, cottons and linens with floral and geometric designs in light, contemporary colours.
Tel: 020 7730 9847

JOHN LEWIS

Department store offering wide selection of fabrics, haberdashery and curtain trimmings.
Tel: 08456 049049
www.johnlewis.co.uk

KNICKERBEAN

Discount stores with designer fabrics at bargain prices.
Tel: 01842 751327

MALABAR

Hand-woven silks and cotton fabrics imported from India.
Tel: 020 7501 4200
www.malabar.co.uk

THE MODERN SAREE CENTRE

Sarees and Indian silks.
Tel: 020 7247 4040

THE NATURAL FABRIC COMPANY

Wide range of natural fabrics from hessian and calico to chambray and sheers.
Tel: 01295 730064
www.naturalfabriccompany.com

OSBORNE & LITTLE

Classic and contemporary prints, weaves and wallpapers.
Tel: 020 7352 1456
www.osborneandlittle.com

WILMAN INTERIORS

Contemporary and classic fabrics and wallpapers.
Tel: 01282 727300
www.wilman.co.uk

BEDLINEN

BEDECK
Bedlinen featuring modern
florals and geometric patterns.
Tel: 0845 603 0861
www.bedeckhome.com

COLOGNE & COTTON
Crisp cotton bedlinen and
pretty duvet covers.
Tel: 01926 332573
www.cologneandcotton.com

COUVERTURE
Hand-embroidered and
appliquéd bedlinen.
Tel: 020 7795 1200
www.couverture.co.uk

DESCAMPS
Quality bedlinen, including
modern patterns and florals.
Tel: 020 7235 6957
www.descamps.com

DORMA
Varied range of bedlinen, from
elaborately classic to plain
contemporary designs.
Tel: 0161 251 4468 for
stockists, 0870 606 6063
for brochure
www.dorma.co.uk

OCEAN
Contemporary bedlinen,
cushions and throws.
Tel: 0870 242 6283
www.oceanuk.com

PEACOCK BLUE
Cotton and linen bedding
including whites, ginghams
and pastels.
Tel: 0870 333 1555

THE WHITE COMPANY
Plain and embroidered
bedlinen in white and cream
made from top-quality linen
and cotton.
Tel: 0870 160 1610
www.thewhiteco.com

YVES DELORME
Luxury French bedlinen in
classic and contemporary
styles.
Tel: 01296 394980
www.yvesdelorme.com

THE BRADLEY COLLECTION
Stylish curtain poles and finials in wood and sleek steel.
Tel: 01449 722724
www.bradleycollection.co.uk

THE CURTAIN EXCHANGE
Quality second-hand curtains bought and sold.
Tel: 020 7731 8316
www.thecurtainexchange.co.uk

ECLECTICS
Made-to-measure and ready-made roller and Roman blinds in smart modern designs.
Tel: 0870 010 2211
www.eclectics.co.uk

JOHN LEWIS
Wide range of fabrics and haberdashery plus curtain-making products.
Tel: 020 7629 7711
www.johnlewis.co.uk

LUXAFLEX
Made-to-measure blinds in modern styles.
Tel: 0161 442 9500
www.luxaflex.com

PRÊT À VIVRE
Curtains and blinds made-to-measure; poles and tiebacks.
Tel: 08451 305161
www.pretavivre.com

ROSEBYS
Ready-made curtains and blinds.
Tel: 0800 052 0493
www.rosebys.com

RUFFLETTE
Tiebacks, blind and eyelet kits and curtain-making products.
Tel: 0161 998 1811
www.rufflette.com

THE SHUTTER SHOP
Wooden shutters made-to-order; wooden Venetian blinds.
Tel: 01252 844575
www.shuttershop.co.uk

WINDOW TREATMENTS

FIREPLACES & FITTINGS

AMAZING GRATES
Reproduction period fireplaces in marble, stone and slate.
Tel: 020 8883 9590

CLAYTON MUNROE
Period-style door handles.
Tel: 01803 762626
www.claytonmunroe.co.uk

ELGIN & HALL
Made-to-order fireplaces in a wide range of styles.
Tel: 01677 450100
www.elgin.co.uk

HAF DESIGNS
Contemporary door handles in steel and brass.
Tel: 01992 505655
www.hafdesigns.co.uk

KNOBS & KNOCKERS
Door furniture in modern and traditional designs.
Tel: 0151 523 4900
www.knobsandknockers.co.uk

RICHARD BURBIDGE
Wooden mouldings for dado rails and panel effects.
Tel: 01691 678201
www.richardburbidge.co.uk

TURNSTYLE DESIGNS
Handcrafted door handles made from resin, pewter and wood.
Tel: 01271 325325
www.turnstyledesigns.com

WINTHER BROWNE
Simple fire surrounds in pine, mahogany and MDF, flatpack ready-to-paint radiator cabinets.
Tel: 020 8803 3434
www.wintherbrowne.co.uk

BUTTERCUPS AND DAISIES
Wide range of floristry
sundries including floral foam,
basketry, craft suppliers and
tools.
Tel: 01202 672200
www.buttercups-daisies.co.uk

BUYRITE
Suppliers of flower pots, raffia,
ribbon and florist's foam.
Tel: 01932 349515
www.buyrite.co.uk

FLORAL PRODUCTS
Specialists in 3D flower
preservation.
Tel: 0800 298 5880
www.flowersforever.co.uk

NOTCUTTS GARDEN CENTRES
Garden centres that also sell
ornaments, features and
furniture. Christmas
Wonderland is on display from
October to December.
Tel: 01394 383344
www.notcutts.co.uk

SMITCRAFT
Suppliers of floristry
accessories, including foam,
ribbons and raffia.
Tel: 01252 342626
www.smitcraft.com

VAN HAGE GARDEN COMPANY
Everything for the garden
under one roof. Also offer a
wide range of Christmas wares.
Tel: 01920 870811
www.vanhage.co.uk

WYEVALE GARDEN CENTRES
Specialist garden centre group.
Tel: 0800 413213 for branches
www.wyevale.co.uk

PAINTS, VARNISHES AND SPECIAL FINISHES

AURO ORGANIC PAINTS
Paints and woodstains made from natural products.
Tel: 01799 543077
www.auroorganic.co.uk

B&Q
Wide range of decorating paints in contemporary colours.
www.diy.com

CRAIG & ROSE
Extensive range of paint in delicious colours.
Tel: 01383 740011

CROWN PAINTS
Decorating and colour advice plus order paint on-line.
Tel: 01254 704951
www.crowntrade.co.uk

DULUX
Wide range of decorating paints in a vast choice of shades.
Tel: 01753 550555
www.dulux.co.uk

FARROW & BALL
Heritage paint shades.
Tel: 01202 876141
www.farrow-ball.co.uk

FIRED EARTH
Neutral and traditional colours.
Tel: 01295 814300
www.firedearth.com

HAMMERITE
Makers of specialist metallic paints and enamels.
Tel: 01661 830000
www.hammerite.com or www.hammerite-automotive.com

HOMEBASE
Tel: 0870 900 8098
www.homebase.co.uk

HUMBROL
Makers of the Glass Etch spray for creating a frosted effect on glass or Perspex. Also makers of chrome paints.
Tel: 01482 701191
www.airfix.com

INTERNATIONAL PAINT

Range of paints, including floor paints and multi-surface primer.
Tel: 01480 484284
www.plascon.co.uk

LIBERON

Makers of gilt cream, waxes and wood finishes.
Tel: 01797 367555

LONDON GRAPHIC CENTRE

Specialist shop offering a range of design sundries, art and craft supplies plus a good selection of handmade papers.
Tel: 020 7759 4500
www.londongraphics.co.uk or www.lgc-online.co.uk/catalogue

PÉBÉO

Craft paints for fabric, glass and porcelain.
Tel: 02380 701144
www.pebeo.com

PLASTI-KOTE

Makers of aerosol spray paints for decorative use, including glass-frosting spray, metallic finishes and sprays suitable for use with stencils.
Tel: 01223 836400
www.spraypaint.co.uk

SANDERSON

More than 1,000 mix-to-order colours in the Spectrum range.
Tel: 01895 830000
www.sanderson-uk.com

ZEST

Vibrant Mediterranean colours.
Tel: 020 7226 6138
www.zestessentials.com

ACCESSORIES

AN ANGEL AT MY TABLE
Pretty painted furniture and
unusual decorative accessories.
Tel: 020 7424 9777

BLISS
Accessories with quirky
shapes, such as clocks.
Tel: 01789 400077
www.blisscatalogue.co.uk

BOMBAY DUCK
Decorative contemporary
accessories, including vases,
photo frames and beaded
items.
Tel: 020 8749 8001
www.bombayduck.co.uk

THE CHRISTMAS SHOP
Sells all things 'Christmassy' for
twelve months of the year.
Tel: 020 7378 1998
www.thechristmasshop.co.uk

THE CONRAN SHOP
Contemporary accessories and
soft furnishings plus storage
items including cookware and
tableware.
Tel: 0870 600 1232
www.conran.co.uk

THE COTSWOLD COMPANY
Country-style storage baskets
in wicker and rattan.
Tel: 01252 391 404
www.cotswoldco.com

THE DORMY HOUSE
Blanket boxes and tables sold
ready-to-paint; headboards
upholstered to order.
Tel: 01264 365789
www.thedormyhouse.com

ELEPHANT
Varied selection of ethnic-style
accessories imported from all
over the world.
Tel: 020 7637 7930

GRAND ILLUSIONS
French country-style furniture,
painted, distressed or waxed.
Tel: 020 8607 9446
www.grandillusions.co.uk

THE HAMBLEDON
Stylish accessories, including
glass and porcelain vases,
soapstone bowls, basketware
and cotton quilts.
Tel: 01962 890055
www.thehambledon.com

FOUND
Candleholders, cushions, picture frames and other accessories, to complement both classic and contemporary looks.
Tel: 0870 166 8131
www.foundat.co.uk

LSA INTERNATIONAL
Wide range of vases, containers and woven baskets.
Tel: 01932 789721
www.lsa-international.com

NEST
A selection of stylish, contemporary vases.
Tel: 01392 204305
www.nestinteriors.com

NEWFRAMES
Sells prints, arty greeting cards, aluminium, ornate, and standard frames to size.
Tel: 020 7437 8881

OKA DIRECT
Oriental-style storage units, chests and side tables in rattan and bamboo.
Tel: 0870 160 6002
www.okadirect.com

PRICE'S CANDLES
Wide range of decorative scented, traditional and garden candles.
Tel: 01234 264 500
www.prices-candles.co.uk

SCUMBLE GOOSIE
Ready-to-paint furniture and accessories including blanks for peg rails, trays and lampbases.
Tel: 01453 731305
www.scumblegoosie.co.uk

SHAKER
Shaker-style wooden furniture, peg rails, oval storage boxes and folk-art accessories.
Tel: 020 7935 9461
www.shaker.co.uk

SUMMERILL & BISHOP
Old and new kitchenware from around the world.
Tel: 020 7221 4566

ONE-STOP SHOPS

ARGOS
Furniture, bedlinen, lighting and accessories.
Tel: 0870 600 3030
www.argos.co.uk

BHS
Furniture, bedlinen, lighting and lighting accessories and fittings.
Tel: 020 7262 3288 for details of your nearest store
www.bhs.co.uk

DEBENHAMS
Furniture, bedlinen, window dressings and lighting.
Tel: 020 7408 4444 for details of your nearest store
www.debenhams.com

FREEMANS
Furniture, bedlinen, window-dressings and lighting.
Tel: 0800 900200
www.freemans.com

HEAL'S
Contemporary accessories.
Tel: 020 7636 1666
www.heals.co.uk

IKEA
Affordable furnishing fabrics and storage accessories.
Tel: 020 8208 5600
www.ikea.co.uk

JOHN LEWIS
A wide range of furniture, fabrics, wallcoverings, bedlinen, lighting and accessories.
Tel: 020 7629 7711 for details of your nearest store
www.johnlewis.co.uk

LAURA ASHLEY
Classic and country-style fabrics, soft furnishings and accessories. Mail order available.
Tel: 0870 562 2116 for stockists or 0800 868 100 for mail order.
www.lauraashley.com

MARKS & SPENCER
A wide range of contemporary and traditional accessories.
Tel: 0845 302 1234
www.marksandspencer.com

MONSOON HOME
Soft furnishings and accessories with an ethnic style.
Tel: 020 7313 3000
www.monsoon.co.uk

MUJI
Japanese-style bowls and dishes, acrylic containers.
Tel: 020 7221 9360
www.muji.co.uk

NEXT HOME
Contemporary furniture, accessories and bedlinen. Mail order available.
Tel: 0870 243 5435 for stockists or 0845 600 7000 for mail order
www.next.co.uk

THE PIER
Reasonably priced accessories and soft furnishings.
Tel: 0845 609 1234
www.pier.co.uk

ONE-STOP SHOPS